INSTANT POT COOKBOOK FOR BEGINNERS:
5 INGREDIENTS OR LESS

By Joan Davis

Contents

INTRODUCTION

Home-cooked meals have a unique power that brings families and friends together. If you tend to make more home-cooked meals, eat healthier and stop spending money on take-outs, the Instant Pot may become your new favorite kitchen gadget. It offers a health-oriented lifestyle to you and your family, it is economical, practical and user-friendly.

According to historical records, Denis Papin, a French physicist, invited one of the earliest pressure cookers, in 1679. In the 70s, pressure cookers started showing up in a large number of households. Those first pressure cookers were different from today. Initially, the pressure cooker was the European answer to the American slow cooker. A pressure cooker has long been an integral part of your grandmother's and great-grandmother's kitchen. It has definitely revolutionized kitchens around the world with its capability to pressure cook a wide variety of food.

In the 19th century, a pressure cooker, as we know it today, took a key step forward in America. In 1991, people started using "third generation" pressure cookers i.e. electric pressure cookers. Nowadays, people around the world cook the best homemade food in their pressure cookers. Swiss households have three pressure cookers on average and almost every U.S. household owns an electric pressure cooker. In fact, every part of the world has its own pressure cooking style with a touch of tradition. The Instant Pot really did "conquer" the whole world!

The Instant Pot is endlessly inspiring and that's the reason why we have so many recipes out there. We could explore this incredible kitchen device for a lifetime and every time we will be stunned by its greatness and versatility. This cookbook will help you to make the most of your new multi-cooker. From appetizing breakfast to side dishes and desserts, you'll learn how to prepare the best one-pot meals ever! This recipe collection is designed to provide pathways to totally new cooking experience; it offers incredibly simple recipes with five ingredients or less! Julia Child, an internationally recognized chef, once said, "Learn how to cook, try new recipes, learn from your mistakes, be fearless, and above all have fun!"

What You Need To Know As a True Pressure Cooker Aficionado

An Instant Pot is a programmable pressure cooker that is designed to use higher temperatures and steam to cook food under pressure. The true power of an Instant Pot is the power to cook food, using an innovative formula, supporting environmental sustainability and global health! It can do the job of a pressure cooker, slow cooker, rice maker, steamer, warming pot, cooking pot, sauté pan, and yogurt maker. Eight different appliances in one kitchen gadget!

How does an Instant Pot work? Simply put, cooking liquids come to a boil under an airtight lid; cooking liquids will turn into a steam shortly thereafter. That super-heated steam produces high pressure inside a cooking chamber, which begins to cook food quickly and evenly.

Simply throw your ingredients into the inner pot. Seal the lid and press the right button. Afterwards, release pressure from your cooker. Bear in mind that "Keep Warm" function will automatically turn on when the cooking cycle has completed.

Manual – use this "multi-purpose" button to adjust the parameters according to your recipe.

Sauté – you can sear the meat, caramelize the onions, and sauté vegetables in your Instant Pot without using any additional pan. Sautéing is one of the easiest flavor-boosting tricks.

Rice – you can cook different types of rice. It takes about 8 minutes to cook 1 cup of white rice; it will take about 25 minutes to cook brown rice and 30 minutes for wild rice.

Multigrain – this fully automated program is perfect for rice and grains.

Poultry – chicken and turkey come out with a perfect, golden skin and juicy, evenly cooked meat.

Slow Cook – a great choice for busy people who want a hot, hearty meal ready when they arrive home.

Meat/Stew – use this program to make budget-friendly cuts of meat as well as hearty stews.

Bean/Chili – you can cook the best bean recipes in no time by using this program.

Steam – this is one of the best ways to get vegetables and seafood onto your plate. Use a metal steam rack or steamer basket.

Soup – use this setting to cook soups, stocks and chowders just like your grandma used to make - without boiling too heavily.

Porridge – you can cook different types of grains and make the best breakfast oatmeal with this useful program.

Yogurt – from now onwards, you can make your own homemade yogurt.

Keep Warm/Cancel – once cooking is done, push the "Cancel" button; otherwise, the warming function will be activated automatically.

How to release pressure? There are two pressure release methods – The quick release method and natural release method.

Quick pressure release – after the cooking process finished, move the venting knob from Sealing position to Venting position. Simple like that!

Natural pressure release – you can leave the valve closed and allow the pressure to decrease on its own; it can take between 10 and 30 minutes; depressurization will depend on how much cooking liquid is in the inner pot. You can also wait only for 10 minutes before realizing any remaining steam. Remember – you can remove the lid when all pressure is released. A quick tip: place a cold towel on the metal portion of the lid to speed up the process.

Must haves for your Instant Pot include Stainless Steel Inner Cooking Pot, Stainless Steel Pressure Cooker Steamer Insert Pans, an extra Silicone Ring, Springform, Pan Glass Lid, Mini Mitts, and a great and reliable Instant Pot Cookbook. It would be great if you can purchase an egg steamer rack, a reusable strainer for making yogurt, and Pyrex glass cups; these accessories can help you get the most out of your Instant Pot. If you are lucky enough to own an Instant pot, you would probably want to check all of its amazing possibilities.

High pressure is default setting on the Instant Pot. On the other hand, you should cook delicate foods such as seafood and eggs on a low-pressure setting.

You can cook almost everything in your Instant Pot, but it can also be a little overwhelming if you're a newbie. With so many buttons, it can be difficult to choose the right cooking program and get the best results in the beginning. However, once you understand how it really works, it's pretty straightforward.

Benefits of an Instant Pot You Need to Know

Using an Instant Pot will give you many benefits. Besides being super delicious, pressure cooked meals are easy to make and fun to eat in many different ways. There's a lot to love about an Instant Pot!

It saves your time and time is priceless.

The main goals of pressure cooking are quality, efficiency, and simplicity. With its all-in-one capability to sauté, slow cook, pasteurize, pressure cook, rice cook, keep warm and more, the Instant Pot saves your time significantly. People love the Instant Pot because it offers comfort food in far less time. Most recipes in this cookbook take about 20 minutes from prep to plate. Simple, speedy, and delicious!

This super-sophisticated machine utilizes a hyper-pressurized environment and automated cooking process to cook your food faster and easier. You can prepare a complete party dinner in your Instant Pot with minimum effort. You can have a no-fuss midweek meal ready in a flash, too. You can also set up this intelligent device to 24-hours in advance. The Instant Pot promotes minimalism, which gives you more time to live a meaningful life.

A smart way to boost your savings.

It wouldn't be wrong to say that the Instant Pot is the best tool to cook economical cuts such as chicken thighs and country-style ribs. It can also keep lean meat like poultry and fish moist and cooked all the way through. Since the Instant Pot uses powerful super-heated pressure, it is clearly evident that Instant Pot uses less energy to cook food. Obviously, it cuts down your electric bill and saves Mother Earth. It is good to know that an Instant Pot allows you to double your recipe, but a larger amount of food does not mean longer cook times; this intelligent device cooks everything at the same rate.

It is a durable cookware so that you can save your money on additional pots and skillets as well. Thanks to your Instant Pot, you and your family can eat well on a budget. This unique-shaped, revolutionary space-saving cookware will save a ton of space in your tiny kitchen. In addition, many recipes call for only few budget-friendly ingredients that are available everywhere.

Health benefits.

Many studies have suggested that cooking in a pressure cooker tends to keep valuable ingredients better than conventional cookware. Airtight lid prevents liquids to escape from the sealed environment, while "trapped" pressure prevents the evaporation. Natural juices are retained rather than boiling away.

The Instant Pot and this recipe collection promote a well-balanced diet with lots of fruits and vegetables, healthy beans and grains, and good fats. It can help you build good cooking habits, lose weight and stay healthy.

5 Ingredient or Less:
Make Every Meal Stress-Free and Delicious

We can describe our recipe collection in a few words: Five ingredients or less, one pot, and lots of fun. How to use an Instant Pot for your cooking needs? For meat eaters, vegetarians or the pickiest eaters in the world, the Instant Pot is actually a common ground. If you tend to simplify things and use as many ingredients as possible, the Instant Pot may become your best friend in the kitchen. Four or five ingredients are all you need to make a filling, super-delicious meals in minutes! An Instant Pot turns every meal into a gastronomical experience. In fact, chefs and culinary experts know how to get the best results through cooking techniques. On the other hand, your Instant Pot can cook almost anything so you do not have to take cooking classes and learn any particular skills. Sound too good to be true? This book will demystify a modern multi-cooker and show you just how useful it can be. Some recipes in this cookbook call for preset times, while others require you to manually set cook time. In this recipe collection, you will learn how to master the art of cooking different foods in your Instant Pot.

MEAT. As for meats, many of us have enjoyed delicious and crispy wings or sticky, perfectly cooked ribs in restaurants. However, when we cook these American Super Bowl classics at home, we end up with a real mess. What should we do for deliciously crispy skin? Luckily, the Instant Pot turns ordinary chicken wings into a five-star gourmet dish! The same goes for ribs and other cuts with skins and bones. If you want to cook a perfect pork roast in your Instant Pot, use the sauté function to sear it for a few minutes. Then, place a metal trivet and water on the bottom of the inner pot; lower pork roast onto the trivet to get it up out of the cooking liquid. Pork is also lovely with an herb crust. Trust us, it comes out perfect every single time!

Finally, if you tend to cook beef, season the meat generously on all sides. Then, use multiple buttons. Firstly, sear the beef for a few minutes per side to lock in flavors; then, choose the "Meat/Stew" function and follow a chart as a guide for cooking times and cook the beef on high pressure. Bear in mind that a thick beef may need to be cooked a little longer so pressure cooking allows tough fibers, collagen and connective tissues to break down inside; it will take between 90 and 120 minutes. Afterwards, when cooking beef, use a slow release of pressure. Always use at least 1/2 to 1 cup of liquid to help your Instant Pot to create a pressure. Simply choose a few common ingredients such as favorite cut of beef, a spice mix, and your favorite vegetables; press the button, and make healthy eating less stressful for you and your family.

VEGETABLES. You can make hearty soups, side dishes and appetizers that are bursting with fresh flavors in no time. We all know that timing is imperative when it comes to perfectly cooked vegetables with vibrant flavors and colors. A steaming rack is a smart cook's secret weapon to cook vegetables that are colorful, crisp, and delicious. One of the greatest benefits of pressure cooking is that super-heated steam will prevent vegetables from getting overcooked. Thanks to the Instant Pot, you can make a hearty soup to feed a family with just five ingredients or less.

DESSERTS. Yes, of course, you can make delectable desserts in the Instant Pot. This cookbook offers the best, hand-picked dessert recipes from a grandma's cookbook. Moreover, they require five ingredients or less.

The Instant Pot will redefine set-it and forget-it meals once and for all. Just crank up your Instant Pot and let the magic begin!

POULTRY

1. Classic Chicken Sandwiches

(Ready in about 20 minutes | Servings 4)

INGREDIENTS

1 pound chicken breasts
4 hamburger buns
4 tablespoons mayonnaise
4 ounces goat cheese, crumbled
1/2 cup tomatoes, sliced

DIRECTIONS

- Season the chicken with salt and black pepper; place the chicken in the Instant Pot. Then, add 1 cup of vegetable stock to the Instant Pot.
- Secure the lid. Choose the "Poultry" setting and cook for 15 minutes under High pressure. Once cooking is complete, use a quick pressure release; carefully remove the lid.
- Assemble your sandwiches with the chicken, hamburger buns, mayo, goat cheese, and tomatoes. You can also add Dijon mustard if desired. Serve and enjoy!

Per serving: 439 Calories; 20.1g Fat; 24.1g Carbs; 38.6g Protein; 4.5g Sugars

2. Greek-Style Chicken Drumsticks

(Ready in about 20 minutes | Servings 4)

INGREDIENTS

1 pound chicken drumsticks
1 cup tomato puree
2 thyme sprigs, chopped
2 garlic cloves, minced

DIRECTIONS

- Season the chicken with salt, ground black pepper, and smoked paprika. Add the chicken to the Instant Pot along with the other ingredients; pour in 1 cup of water and gently stir to combine well.
- Secure the lid. Choose the "Poultry" setting and cook for 15 minutes under High pressure. Once cooking is complete, use a quick pressure release; carefully remove the lid.
- You can thicken the sauce on the "Sauté" setting for a couple of minutes if desired.
- Divide the chicken drumsticks among serving plates. Top with the sauce. Garnish with rosemary and Kalamata olives if desired. Enjoy!

Per serving: 273 Calories; 14.4g Fat; 8.5g Carbs; 27.6g Protein; 3.6g Sugars

3. Mexican-Style Turkey Tacos

(Ready in about 15 minutes | Servings 6)

INGREDIENTS

2 pounds turkey breasts
2 garlic cloves, smashed
1/4 cup fresh cilantro leaves, chopped
6 corn tortillas, warmed
1 cup Pico de Gallo

DIRECTIONS

- Put the turkey breast into your Instant Pot. Now, pour in 1 cup of water. Sprinkle with salt, black pepper, and red pepper. Add garlic and cilantro leaves.
- Secure the lid. Choose the "Manual" setting and cook for 10 minutes at High pressure.
- Once cooking is complete, use a natural release and carefully remove the lid. Shred the turkey breasts.
- Serve the shredded turkey breasts over corn tortillas garnished with Pico de Gallo. Bon appétit!

Per serving: 323 Calories; 12g Fat; 15.2g Carbs; 37.1g Protein; 2.8g Sugars

4. Tender Four-Cheese Italian Chicken

(Ready in about 15 minutes | Servings 4)

INGREDIENTS

3 garlic cloves, minced

2 rosemary sprigs, leaves picked

2 ripe tomatoes, chopped

4 chicken fillets, boneless and skinless

1/2 cup 4-Cheese Italian, shredded

DIRECTIONS

- Press the "Sauté" button to heat up your Instant Pot. Now, melt 1 tablespoon of butter.
- Add the garlic and rosemary, and sauté until they are fragrant.
- Now, stir in the chopped tomatoes. Season the chicken fillets with salt, ground pepper, and paprika. You can add curry powder if desired.
- Add the chicken fillets to the Instant Pot. Then, pour in water to cover the chicken.
- Secure the lid and select the "Poultry" mode. Cook for 6 minutes. Once cooking is complete, use a natural release and carefully remove the lid.
- Press the "Sauté" button. Add shredded cheese and cook 2 to 3 minutes more or until cheese is melted. Serve right away garnished with fresh chopped chives. Bon appétit!

Per serving: 193 Calories; 12.5g Fat; 5g Carbs; 15.8g Protein; 2.3g Sugars

5. Capellini with Chicken and Cream

(Ready in about 15 minutes | Servings 4)

INGREDIENTS

1 pound chicken breasts, chopped
2 garlic cloves, minced
1 cup double cream + 1/3 cup milk
10 ounces capellini (or your favorite type of pasta)
1/2 cup Parmigiano-Reggiano cheese, grated

DIRECTIONS

- Press the "Sauté" button to preheat your Instant Pot. Heat 2 tablespoons of oil until sizzling. Now, sear the chicken until it is delicately browned; reserve.
- Then, add the garlic and continue to sauté an additional 30 seconds or until it is fragrant. Season with salt and freshly ground black pepper; add the cream and milk.
- Bring to a simmer and press the "Cancel" button. Pour in 2 ½ cups water or vegetable broth; afterwards, add the pasta.
- Secure the lid. Choose the "Manual" mode and cook for 8 minutes under High pressure. Once cooking is complete, use a natural pressure release; carefully remove the lid.
- Top with Parmigiano-Reggiano cheese and serve immediately with fresh lemon wedges if desired. Enjoy!

Per serving: 537 Calories; 33.3g Fat; 26.9g Carbs; 33.3g Protein; 5.3g Sugars

6. Bourbon Chicken Liver Pâté

(Ready in about 10 minutes | Servings 8)

INGREDIENTS

3/4 pound chicken livers, trimmed
1/2 cup onions, chopped
2/3 cup chicken stock
3 tablespoons bourbon
1/2 cup heavy cream

DIRECTIONS

- Press the "Sauté" button to preheat your Instant Pot; melt 2 tablespoons of butter. Sear the chicken livers for 3 minutes per side.
- Add the onions, chicken stock, bourbon, and heavy cream to your Instant Pot.
- Season with the oregano, ground allspice, salt, black pepper, and marjoram.
- Secure the lid. Choose the "Manual" mode and High pressure; cook for 3 minutes. Once cooking is complete, use a quick pressure release; carefully remove the lid.
- Purée the mixture in a food processor until smooth. Transfer to a serving bowl and garnish with sage sprigs. Bon appétit!

Per serving: 180 Calories; 7.9g Fat; 1.2g Carbs; 23.6g Protein; 0.5g Sugars

7. Turkey and Tomato Soup

(Ready in about 25 minutes | Servings 5)

INGREDIENTS

1 medium-sized leek, chopped
1 (28-ounce) can diced tomatoes
1 celery stalk, chopped
1 carrot, chopped
1 pound turkey thighs

DIRECTIONS

- Press the "Sauté" button to preheat your Instant Pot. Heat 1 tablespoon of peanut oil until sizzling. Cook the leek until tender.
- Add the remaining ingredients; add 5 cups of water or broth.
- Secure the lid. Choose the "Soup" setting and cook for 20 minutes at High pressure. Once cooking is complete, use a quick pressure release; carefully remove the lid.
- Remove the turkey thighs from the soup, shred the meat and discard the bones. After that, return the meat to the Instant Pot.
- Divide among five soup bowls. Top each bowl with fresh coriander for garnish and serve immediately.

Per serving: 194 Calories; 7.9g Fat; 12.7g Carbs; 18.8g Protein; 7.4g Sugars

BEEF

8. Shoulder Roast with Potatoes and Pepperoncini

(Ready in about 45 minutes | Servings 8)

INGREDIENTS

3 pounds shoulder roast
1 teaspoon ginger garlic paste
1 ½ cups vegetable broth
4 pepperoncini peppers
2 pounds russet potatoes, peeled and quartered

DIRECTIONS

- Press the "Sauté" button to preheat your Instant Pot. Now, melt 1 tablespoon of tallow. Sear the roast until it is delicately browned on all sides.
- Add the ginger garlic paste. Sprinkle with salt, pepper, and ranch dressing mix. Pour in vegetable broth. Top with the pepperoncini peppers.
- Secure the lid. Choose the "Meat/Stew" mode and High pressure; cook for 35 minutes. Once cooking is complete, use a natural pressure release; carefully remove the lid. Shred the meat with two forks.
- Add the potatoes and secure the lid. Choose "Manual" mode and High pressure; cook for 5 minutes. Once cooking is complete, use a quick pressure release; carefully remove the lid.
- Serve the pulled beef with the potatoes and enjoy!

Per serving: 313 Calories; 8.1g Fat; 24.8g Carbs; 34.6g Protein; 3.1g Sugars

9. Hearty Ground Beef Soup

(Ready in about 25 minutes | Servings 4)

INGREDIENTS

1 pound ground beef
1 onion, peeled and finely chopped
1 parsnip, thinly sliced
2 carrots, thinly sliced
1/2 cup tomato purée

DIRECTIONS

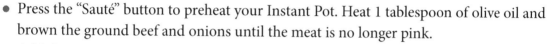

- Press the "Sauté" button to preheat your Instant Pot. Heat 1 tablespoon of olive oil and brown the ground beef and onions until the meat is no longer pink.
- Add the remaining ingredients to your Instant Pot. Season with salt, ground black pepper, cayenne pepper, and garlic powder. Pour in 4 cups of water or beef bone broth.
- Secure the lid. Choose the "Soup" mode and High pressure; cook for 20 minutes. Once cooking is complete, use a quick pressure release; carefully remove the lid.
- Ladle into individual bowls and serve hot. Bon appétit!

Per serving: 340 Calories; 16.3g Fat; 15.7g Carbs; 31.9g Protein; 7.2g Sugars

10. Autumn Roast with Vegetables

(Ready in about 55 minutes | Servings 6)

INGREDIENTS

2 pounds beef roast
1/2 cup Chianti
1 cup shallots, chopped
2 cloves garlic, pressed
3 carrots, sliced

DIRECTIONS

- Press the "Sauté" button to preheat your Instant Pot. Heat 2 tablespoons of olive oil and brown the beef for 4 to 5 minutes.
- Add the Chianti, shallots, and garlic to the Instant Pot. Pour in 1 cup of water. Sprinkle with salt and pepper to taste. You can add 2 bay leaves if desired.
- Secure the lid. Choose the "Meat/Stew" mode and High pressure; cook for 45 minutes. Once cooking is complete, use a quick pressure release; carefully remove the lid.
- Then, add the carrots to the Instant Pot.
- Secure the lid. Choose the "Manual" mode and High pressure; cook for 5 minutes. Once cooking is complete, use a quick pressure release; carefully remove the lid.
- You can thicken the cooking liquid on "Sauté" function if desired. Bon appétit!

Per serving: 363 Calories; 17.6g Fat; 6.1g Carbs; 41.6g Protein; 1.8g Sugars

11. Beef Brisket with Monterey Jack Cheese

(Ready in about 1 hour 5 minutes | Servings 6)

INGREDIENTS

2 pounds beef brisket

2 garlic cloves, chopped

1 leek, chopped

1 cup Monterey Jack cheese, freshly grated

DIRECTIONS

- Press the "Sauté" button to preheat your Instant Pot. Then, melt 2 tablespoons of lard.
- Once hot, sear the brisket for 2 to 3 minutes on each side. Sauté the garlic and leek in pan drippings.
- Then, add spices to taste. Pour in 1 cup of water or a homemade beef bone broth.
- Secure the lid. Choose the "Manual" mode and High pressure; cook for 60 minutes. Once cooking is complete, use a natural pressure release; carefully remove the lid.
- Slice the beef into strips and top with cheese.
- Press the "Sauté" button once again and allow it to simmer until cheese is melted. Serve warm.

Per serving: 434 Calories; 33.7g Fat; 3.2g Carbs; 28g Protein; 0.7g Sugars

12. Sirloin Steak with Hoisin Sauce

(Ready in about 1 hour | Servings 8)

INGREDIENTS

2 pounds boneless sirloin steak, thinly sliced
1/2 cup red onion, sliced
2 garlic cloves, minced
2 sweet peppers, deveined and sliced
1/2 cup hoisin sauce

DIRECTIONS

- Press the "Sauté" button and preheat the Instant Pot; melt 1 tablespoon of lard. Once hot, brown the sirloin steak for 6 minutes, flipping halfway through cooking time. Season the steak with salt, black pepper, chili powder, and parsley.
- Add the onion, garlic, and peppers. Pour in 1 cup of water or a homemade beef broth.
- Secure the lid. Select "Manual" setting, High pressure and 50 minutes. Once cooking is complete, use a natural release and carefully remove the lid.
- Shred the beef and return it to the Instant Pot; stir to combine. Afterwards, pour the hoisin sauce over shredded beef and vegetables and serve immediately. Bon appétit!

Per serving: 283 Calories; 14.9g Fat; 10.9g Carbs; 24.8g Protein; 4.6g Sugars

13. Steak and Tomato Soup

(Ready in about 25 minutes | Servings 4)

INGREDIENTS

1 pound beef steak, cut into cubes
2 (8-ounce) cans tomato sauce
1 package prepared mixed vegetables (soup mix)
2 cloves garlic, minced
1 bay leaf

DIRECTIONS

- Simply throw all of the above ingredients into your Instant Pot that is previously greased with a nonstick cooking spray.
- Pour in 4 cups of water.
- Secure the lid. Choose the "Soup" mode and High pressure; cook for 20 minutes. Once cooking is complete, use a quick pressure release; carefully remove the lid.
- Divide the soup among four serving bowls and serve warm.

Per serving: 278 Calories; 7.6g Fat; 22.3g Carbs; 30.4g Protein; 9.7g Sugars

14. Saucy Rice with Ground Beef

(Ready in about 15 minutes | Servings 4)

INGREDIENTS

1/2 cup leeks, chopped
1 (1-inch) piece ginger root, peeled and grated
1 ½ pounds ground chuck
1 cup tomato purée
2 cups Arborio rice

DIRECTIONS

- Press the "Sauté" button to preheat your Instant Pot. Now, heat 1 tablespoon of sesame oil and sauté the leeks and ginger root until tender.
- Then, add the ground chuck; cook for 1 minute more. Season with salt, black pepper, and red pepper flakes.
- Add the tomato puree and 1 ½ cups of water. Stir in rice.
- Secure the lid. Choose the "Manual" mode and High pressure; cook for 7 minutes. Once cooking is complete, use a quick pressure release; carefully remove the lid. Serve immediately.

Per serving: 493 Calories; 28.8g Fat; 34.9g Carbs; 42.1g Protein; 3.3g Sugars

15. Classic Italian Pepperonata

(Ready in about 1 hour 10 minutes | Servings 6)

INGREDIENTS

2 pounds top round steak, cut into bite-sized chunks
1 red onion, chopped
1 pound mixed bell peppers, deveined and thinly sliced
2 cloves garlic, minced
1/2 cup dry red wine

DIRECTIONS

- Press the "Sauté" button to preheat your Instant Pot. Then, melt 2 teaspoons of lard. Cook the round steak approximately 5 minutes, stirring periodically; reserve.
- Then, sauté the onion for 2 minutes or until translucent.
- Stir in the remaining ingredients. Season with Italian seasoning blend, sea salt ground black pepper, and salt-packed capers. Pour in 1 cup of water.
- Secure the lid. Choose the "Manual" mode and High pressure; cook for 60 minutes. Once cooking is complete, use a natural pressure release; carefully remove the lid. Bon appétit!

Per serving: 309 Calories; 7.4g Fat; 10.8g Carbs; 46.9g Protein; 5.1g Sugars

PORK

16. Barbeque Pork Butt Roast

(Ready in about 30 minutes | Servings 6)

INGREDIENTS

3 pounds pork butt roast
1 cup ketchup
1/4 cup champagne vinegar
3 tablespoons brown sugar
1 teaspoon ground mustard

DIRECTIONS

- Add all of the above ingredients to your Instant Pot. Season with salt, black pepper, and garlic powder.
- Pour 1 cup of water over the pork butt roast.
- Secure the lid and select the "Meat/Stew" mode. Cook for 20 minutes under High pressure. Once cooking is complete, use a natural pressure release; carefully remove the lid.
- Shred the meat and return it back to the Instant Pot. Serve the pork with the sauce and enjoy!

Per serving: 435 Calories; 18.9g Fat; 15.1g Carbs; 48.8g Protein; 12.4g Sugars

17. Pork Cutlets with Ricotta Sauce

(Ready in about 15 minutes | Servings 4)

INGREDIENTS

2 chicken bouillon cubes
2 cloves garlic, finely chopped
1 pound pork cutlets
6 ounces Ricotta cheese

DIRECTIONS

- Add the bouillon cubes and garlic to the Instant Pot. Pour in 1 cup of water.
- Season the pork cutlets with salt, black pepper, and cayenne pepper and place them in the Instant Pot.
- Secure the lid. Choose the "Manual" setting and cook at High pressure for 8 minutes. Once cooking is complete, use a quick pressure release; carefully remove the lid.
- Then, whisk 1 ½ tablespoons of cornstarch and 2 tablespoons of water in a mixing bowl to make a slurry; add the slurry to the cooking liquid.
- Press the "Sauté" button and let it cook until thickened. Afterwards, fold in the Ricotta cheese and serve immediately. Bon appétit!

Per serving: 334 Calories; 18.3g Fat; 5.8g Carbs; 34.2g Protein; 0.4g Sugars

18. Sticky Pork Belly with Mustard

(Ready in about 50 minutes | Servings 8)

INGREDIENTS

1 teaspoon garlic paste
1 ½ pounds pork belly, scored and patted dry
1/2 dry white wine
3 tablespoons maple syrup
1/2 teaspoon ground allspice

DIRECTIONS

- Spread the garlic paste over the pork belly; sprinkle with salt, black pepper, dried marjoram, stone-ground mustard, and red pepper flakes to your taste.
- Press the "Sauté" button to preheat your Instant Pot. Then, sear the pork belly for 3 minutes per side.
- In a mixing bowl, thoroughly combine the wine, maple syrup, and allspice; add 1 cup of water. Pour this mixture over the pork belly in the Instant Pot.
- Secure the lid. Choose the "Meat/Stew" setting and cook at High pressure for 40 minutes. Once cooking is complete, use a natural pressure release; carefully remove the lid.
- Cut the prepared pork belly into pieces; serve with some extra mustard, if desired. Bon appétit!

Per serving: 475 Calories; 45.1g Fat; 6.1g Carbs; 8.1g Protein; 4.9g Sugars

19. Pork Steaks with Herbs

(Ready in about 15 minutes | Servings 6)

INGREDIENTS

1 ½ pounds pork steaks
1 cup roasted vegetable broth
2 sprigs rosemary
1 sprig thyme
1 tablespoon fresh parsley

DIRECTIONS

- Press the "Sauté" button to preheat your Instant Pot; melt 2 teaspoons of lard. Once hot, sear the pork until delicately browned.
- Stir in the remaining ingredients. Sprinkle with salt and mixed peppercorns to taste.
- Secure the lid. Choose the "Manual" setting and cook at High pressure for 8 minutes. Once cooking is complete, use a quick pressure release; carefully remove the lid.
- Press the "Sauté" button to thicken the sauce. Serve warm and enjoy!

Per serving: 476 Calories; 44.2g Fat; 0.1g Carbs; 21.2g Protein; 0.1g Sugars

20. Pork Ribs with Honey and Beer

(Ready in about 30 minutes | Servings 8)

INGREDIENTS

2 pounds pork ribs

1 cup tomato paste

1 (12-ounce) bottle light beer

1 tablespoon honey

1 tablespoon ground cumin

DIRECTIONS

- Add all the ingredients to your Instant Pot.
- Season the pork with salt, black pepper, garlic powder, shallot powder, cumin, and paprika to your taste. Pour in 1 cup of water or beef bone broth.
- Secure the lid. Choose the "Meat/Stew" setting and cook at High pressure for 20 minutes. Once cooking is complete, use a natural pressure release; carefully remove the lid.
- Serve over roasted potatoes and enjoy!

Per serving: 268 Calories; 8.9g Fat; 19.7g Carbs; 26.7g Protein; 15.1g Sugars

21. Colorful Pork and Vegetable Soup

(Ready in about 40 minutes | Servings 4)

INGREDIENTS

1 tablespoon olive oil
1 pound pork stew meat, cubed
1 (28-ounce) package mixed vegetables for soup
4 cups beef bone broth
2 cups spinach

DIRECTIONS

- Press the "Sauté" button to preheat your Instant Pot; heat 1 tablespoon of oil. Now, sear the meat until it is delicately browned.
- Add the mixed vegetables for the soup and beef bone broth. Sprinkle with salt and black pepper.
- Secure the lid. Choose the "Soup" setting and cook at High pressure for 30 minutes. Once cooking is complete, use a quick pressure release; carefully remove the lid.
- Add the spinach to the Instant Pot; seal the lid and allow it to sit in the residual heat until wilted.
- Ladle the soup into individual bowls and serve right away. Bon appétit!

Per serving: 264 Calories; 8.6g Fat; 6.6g Carbs; 38.2g Protein; 2.5g Sugars

22. Pork in Sweet Wine Sauce

(Ready in about 30 minutes | Servings 6)

INGREDIENTS

2 pounds pork shoulder, cut into four pieces
2 garlic cloves, chopped
2 tablespoons honey
1/2 cup Riesling
1 tablespoon Worcestershire sauce

DIRECTIONS

- Press the "Sauté" button to preheat your Instant Pot. Melt 2 tablespoons of lard. Then, sear the meat for 2 to 3 minutes, stirring frequently.
- Add the garlic, honey, Riesling, and Worcestershire sauce to the Instant Pot.
- Pour in 1 cup of water and gently stir to combine. Add the rosemary, thyme, salt and black pepper to taste.
- Secure the lid. Choose the "Meat/Stew" setting and cook at High pressure for 20 minutes. Once cooking is complete, use a quick pressure release; carefully remove the lid. Bon appétit!

Per serving: 483 Calories; 31g Fat; 7.3g Carbs; 38g Protein; 6.1g Sugars

23. Barbecued Pulled Pork with Apples

(Ready in about 35 minutes | Servings 8)

INGREDIENTS

2 ½ pounds pork butt, cut into bite-sized cubes
1/2 cup barbecue sauce
1 tablespoon maple syrup
1 red chili pepper, minced
1 cooking apple, cored and diced

DIRECTIONS

- Add the pork, barbecue sauce, maple syrup, chili pepper, and apple to your Instant Pot.
- Season with salt, black pepper, oregano, basil. Pour in 1 cup of water or a homemade vegetable broth.
- Secure the lid. Choose the "Soup" setting and cook at High pressure for 30 minutes. Once cooking is complete, use a natural pressure release; carefully remove the lid.
- Shred the pork with two forks. Return it back to the Instant Pot. Serve with lemon slices. Bon appétit!

Per serving: 434 Calories; 25.2g Fat; 13.6g Carbs; 36.1g Protein; 10.5g Sugars

FISH & SEAFOOD

24. Tuna with Parsley and Eschalots

(Ready in about 10 minutes | Servings 4)

INGREDIENTS

2 lemons, 1 whole and 1 freshly squeezed
1 pound tuna fillets
1 tablespoon dried parsley flakes
2 tablespoons butter, melted
2 eschalots, thinly sliced

DIRECTIONS

- Place 1 cup of water and lemon juice in the Instant Pot. Add a steamer basket too. Season the tuna fillets with salt and pepper.
- Place the tuna fillets in the steamer basket. Then, sprinkle the dried parsley flakes over the fish; drizzle with butter and top with the thinly sliced eschalots.
- Secure the lid. Choose the "Steam" mode and Low pressure; cook for 3 minutes. Once cooking is complete, use a quick pressure release; carefully remove the lid.
- Serve immediately with lemon. Bon appétit!

Per serving: 249 Calories; 9.1g Fat; 11.7g Carbs; 29.5g Protein; 5.6g Sugars

25. Pilaf with Herbs and Carp

(Ready in about 15 minutes | Servings 4)

INGREDIENTS

1 pound carp, chopped
1 cup tomato paste
1 teaspoon dried rosemary, crushed
1/2 teaspoon dried marjoram leaves
1 cup Arborio rice

DIRECTIONS

- Press the "Sauté" button to preheat your Instant Pot. Heat 1 tablespoon of olive oil. Then, cook the carp for 2 to 3 minutes.
- Season the carp with sea salt and ground black pepper to taste. Add the tomato paste, rosemary, marjoram and rice to the Instant Pot.
- Lastly, pour in 1 cup of water or chicken stock.
- Secure the lid. Choose the "Manual" mode and High pressure; cook for 6 minutes. Once cooking is complete, use a quick pressure release; carefully remove the lid.
- Serve in individual serving bowls, garnished with fresh parsley and oregano leaves.

Per serving: 336 Calories; 16.7g Fat; 28.4g Carbs; 28.6g Protein; 8.8g Sugars

26. Delicious Tilapia with Mushrooms

(Ready in about 15 minutes | Servings 3)

INGREDIENTS

3 tilapia fillets
1 cup Cremini mushrooms, thinly sliced
1/2 cup yellow onions, sliced
2 cloves garlic, peeled and minced
2 tablespoons avocado oil

DIRECTIONS

- Season the tilapia fillets with salt, black pepper, and cayenne pepper on all sides. Place the tilapia fillets in the steaming basket fitted for your Instant Pot.
- Place the sliced mushroom and yellow onions on top of the fillets. Place the garlic and avocado oil over everything.
- Add 1 ½ cups of water to the base of your Instant Pot. Add the steaming basket to the Instant Pot and secure the lid.
- Select the "Manual" mode. Cook for 8 minutes at Low pressure. Once cooking is complete, use a quick release; remove the lid carefully. Garnish with thyme and rosemary.
- Serve immediately.

Per serving: 218 Calories; 12.9g Fat; 2.2g Carbs; 23.6g Protein; 0.7g Sugars

27. Shrimp in Herbed Tomato Sauce

(Ready in about 15 minutes | Servings 4)

INGREDIENTS

1 cup green onions, chopped

1 teaspoon garlic, minced

1 ½ pounds shrimp, peeled and deveined

1 tablespoon tamari sauce

2 ripe tomatoes, chopped

DIRECTIONS

- Press the "Sauté" button to preheat your Instant Pot. Melt 1 tablespoon of butter and cook the green onions until they have softened.
- Now, stir in the garlic and cook an additional 30 seconds or until it is aromatic. Add the rest of the above ingredients.
- Secure the lid. Choose the "Manual" mode and Low pressure; cook for 3 minutes. Once cooking is complete, use a quick pressure release; carefully remove the lid.
- Serve over hot jasmine rice, garnished with thyme and rosemary. Enjoy!

Per serving: 214 Calories; 5.4g Fat; 3.9g Carbs; 35.5g Protein; 2.5g Sugars

28. Fisherman's Risotto with Sea Bass

(Ready in about 10 minutes | Servings 4)

INGREDIENTS

1/2 cup leeks, sliced
2 cups basmati rice
1 ½ pounds sea bass fillets, diced

DIRECTIONS

- Press the "Sauté" button to preheat your Instant Pot. Then, melt 2 tablespoons of butter and sweat the leeks for 2 to 3 minutes.
- Add the rice and sea bass fillets to the Instant Pot. Season the fish fillets with salt, pepper, and ginger to taste. Lastly, pour in 1 cup of water or a homemade roasted-vegetable broth.
- Secure the lid. Choose the "Manual" mode and Low pressure; cook for 4 minutes. Once cooking is complete, use a quick pressure release; carefully remove the lid.
- Serve warm in individual bowls and enjoy!

Per serving: 432 Calories; 22.2g Fat; 32.2g Carbs; 42g Protein; 1.1g Sugars

29. Parmesan Crusted Baked Fish

(Ready in about 15 minutes | Servings 4)

INGREDIENTS

2 ripe tomatoes, sliced

1 teaspoon rosemary

4 mahi-mahi fillets

2 tablespoons butter, at room temperature

8 ounces Parmesan cheese, freshly grated

DIRECTIONS

- Add 1 ½ cups of water and a metal rack to your Instant Pot.
- Spritz a casserole dish with a nonstick cooking spray. Arrange the slices of tomatoes on the bottom of the dish. Sprinkle with rosemary.
- Place the mahi-mahi fillets on the top; drizzle the melted butter over the fish. Season it with salt and black pepper to taste. Place the baking dish on the rack.
- Secure the lid. Choose the "Manual" mode and Low pressure; cook for 9 minutes. Once cooking is complete, use a quick pressure release; carefully remove the lid.
- Top with parmesan and seal the lid again; allow the cheese to melt and serve.

Per serving: 376 Calories; 22.1g Fat; 9.4g Carbs; 34.2g Protein; 0.8g Sugars

30. Grouper with Lemon Butter

(Ready in about 15 minutes | Servings 4)

INGREDIENTS

4 grouper fillets
4 tablespoons butter
2 tablespoons fresh lemon juice
2 garlic cloves, smashed

DIRECTIONS

- Add 1 ½ cups of water and a steamer basket to the Instant Pot. Then, place the fish fillets in the steamer basket.
- Add the butter, lemon juice, and garlic. Season with paprika, salt, and black pepper.
- Secure the lid. Choose the "Manual" mode and Low pressure; cook for 4 minutes. Once cooking is complete, use a quick pressure release; carefully remove the lid. Serve immediately.

Per serving: 344 Calories; 14.1g Fat; 1.1g Carbs; 50.1g Protein; 0.2g Sugars

31. Mackerel Fillets with Peppers

(Ready in about 15 minutes | Servings 5)

INGREDIENTS

5 mackerel fillets, skin on
Sea salt and ground black pepper, to taste
1 tablespoon butter, melted
1 red bell pepper, deveined and sliced
1 green bell pepper, deveined and sliced

DIRECTIONS

- Prepare your Instant Pot by adding 1 ½ cups of water and a steamer basket to its bottom.
- Season the mackerel fillets with the salt, black pepper, cayenne pepper, rosemary, and marjoram.
- Place the mackerel fillets in the steamer basket. Drizzle with the melted butter. Top with the sliced peppers.
- Secure the lid and choose the "Manual" setting. Cook for 3 minutes at Low pressure. Once cooking is complete, use a quick release; carefully remove the lid. Serve immediately.

Per serving: 423 Calories; 7.9g Fat; 1.6g Carbs; 80g Protein; 0.9g Sugars

VEGETABLES & SIDE DISHES

32. Easy Sweet Potatoes with Butter

(Ready in about 35 minutes | Servings 4)

INGREDIENTS

1 pound whole small sweet potatoes, cleaned
1/4 teaspoon salt
1/4 teaspoon freshly grated nutmeg
2 tablespoons light butter

DIRECTIONS

- Add 1 cup of water and a steamer basket to the Instant Pot. Arrange the sweet potatoes in the steamer basket.
- Secure the lid and choose the "Steam" mode. Cook for 10 minutes under High pressure. Once cooking is complete, use a natural release for 20 minutes; carefully remove the lid.
- Toss the steamed sweet potatoes with salt, nutmeg, and butter. Eat warm. Bon appétit!

Per serving: 154 Calories; 5.9g Fat; 23.5g Carbs; 2.3g Protein; 7.3g Sugars

33. Sesame Bok Choy with Kalamata Olives

(Ready in about 10 minutes | Servings 4)

INGREDIENTS

1 pound Bok choy, leaves separated
2 teaspoons canola oil
3 tablespoons black sesame seeds
2 tablespoons soy sauce
1/2 cup Kalamata olives, pitted and sliced

DIRECTIONS

- Prepare the Instant Pot by adding 1 ½ cups of water and a steamer basket to the bottom. Place the Bok choy in the steamer basket.
- Secure the lid. Select the "Manual" mode and cook for 4 minutes under High pressure. Once cooking is complete, use a quick pressure release; carefully remove the lid.
- Transfer the Bok choy to a bowl and toss with the remaining ingredients. Season them with smoked paprika, salt, and black pepper to taste. Bon appétit!

Per serving: 178 Calories; 10.8g Fat; 14.3g Carbs; 12.8g Protein; 2.1g Sugars

34. Broccoli with Cheesy Chili Dip

(Ready in about 15 minutes | Servings 6)

INGREDIENTS

1 ½ pounds broccoli, broken into florets
For the Sauce:
1 (15-ounces) can of chili
1 cup Ricotta cheese, crumbled
1 ¼ cups Gruyère cheese shredded
1/4 cup salsa

DIRECTIONS

- Add 1 cup of water to the base of your Instant Pot.
- Put the broccoli florets into the steaming basket. Transfer the steaming basket to the Instant Pot.
- Secure the lid. Choose the "Manual" mode and High pressure; cook for 3 minutes. Once cooking is complete, use a quick pressure release; carefully remove the lid.
- Now, cook all the sauce ingredients in a sauté pan that is preheated over medium-low flame. Cook for 7 minutes or until everything is incorporated.
- Serve the steamed broccoli with the sauce on the side. Bon appétit!

Per serving: 246 Calories; 14.5g Fat; 13.6g Carbs; 17.1g Protein; 2.8g Sugars

35. Sweet Potatoes with Romano Cheese

(Ready in about 15 minutes | Servings 4)

INGREDIENTS

1 ½ pounds sweet potatoes, cubed
1/2 cup spring onions, roughly chopped
2 tablespoons extra-virgin olive oil
1/2 cup Romano cheese, freshly grated
1/2 teaspoon cayenne pepper

DIRECTIONS

- Pour 1 cup of water into the base of your Instant Pot. Put the sweet potatoes into the steaming basket. Transfer the steaming basket to the Instant Pot.
- Secure the lid and choose the "Manual" button, High pressure and 9 minutes. Once cooking is complete, use a natural release; carefully remove the lid.
- Toss the warm potatoes with the spring onions, olive oil, Romano cheese, and cayenne pepper. Season with salt and black pepper to your liking. Serve immediately and enjoy!

Per serving: 109 Calories; 5.9g Fat; 10g Carbs; 5.6g Protein; 0.2g Sugars

36. Steamed Green Beans with Pancetta

(Ready in about 10 minutes | Servings 4)

INGREDIENTS

2 garlic cloves, pressed
1 yellow onion, chopped
5 ounces pancetta, diced
1 ½ pounds green beans, cut in half

DIRECTIONS

- Press the "Sauté" button to heat up your Instant Pot. Now, heat 2 tablespoons of sesame oil and sauté the garlic and onion until softened and fragrant; set it aside.
- After that, stir in the pancetta and continue to cook for a further 4 minutes; crumble with a fork and set it aside.
- Now, throw the green beans into your Instant Pot. Pour in 1 cup of water.
- Secure the lid. Choose the "Manual" mode and Low pressure; cook for 3 minutes. Once cooking is complete, use a quick pressure release; carefully remove the lid.
- Serve warm, garnished with the reserved onion/garlic mixture and pancetta. Bon appétit!

Per serving: 177 Calories; 12.1g Fat; 9.9g Carbs; 8.8g Protein; 2.3g Sugars

37. Creamy Coconut Celery Soup

(Ready in about 10 minutes | Servings 4)

INGREDIENTS

1 teaspoon garlic, minced
1/2 cup leeks, chopped
1 pound celery with leaves, chopped
1 (2-inch) piece young galangal, peeled and chopped
1/2 cup coconut cream, unsweetened

DIRECTIONS

- Press the "Sauté" button to heat up your Instant Pot. Heat 1 tablespoon of sesame oil and sauté the garlic and leeks until tender, about 1 minute 30 seconds.
- Stir in the celery and galangal; continue to cook for a further 2 minutes.
- Next pour in 4 cups of roasted vegetable stock (preferably homemade).
- Secure the lid. Choose the "Manual" mode and High pressure; cook for 3 minutes. Once cooking is complete, use a quick pressure release; carefully remove the lid.
- Then, purée the soup with an immersion blender until smooth and creamy. Return the pureed soup to the Instant Pot; fold in the coconut cream.
- Afterwards, press the "Sauté" button. Allow your soup to simmer until thoroughly warmed. Ladle into soup bowls and serve hot. Bon appétit!

Per serving: 200 Calories; 15.9g Fat; 9.5g Carbs; 7.7g Protein; 3.7g Sugars

38. Brussels Sprouts with Scallions and Cheese

(Ready in about 15 minutes | Servings 4)

INGREDIENTS

1 ½ pounds Brussels sprouts, trimmed
3 tablespoons ghee
2 garlic cloves, minced
1/2 cup scallions, finely chopped
1 cup Romano cheese, grated

DIRECTIONS

- Place 1 cup of water and a steamer basket on the bottom of your Instant Pot. Place the Brussels sprouts in the steamer basket.
- Secure the lid. Choose the "Steam" mode and High pressure; cook for 5 minutes. Once cooking is complete, use a quick pressure release; carefully remove the lid.
- While the Brussels sprouts are still hot, add the ghee, garlic, scallions, and Romano cheese. Season Brussels sprouts with salt, black pepper, and red pepper. Toss to coat well and serve.

Per serving: 261 Calories; 16.2g Fat; 20.1g Carbs; 13.2g Protein; 4.1g Sugars

39. Classic Carrot Puree

(Ready in about 10 minutes | Servings 6)

INGREDIENTS

2 pounds carrots, chopped
2 tablespoons butter, room temperature
1 teaspoon paprika
1 teaspoon coriander
1/4 cup heavy cream

DIRECTIONS

- Add 1 cup of water to the base of your Instant Pot.
- Put the carrots into the steaming basket. Transfer the steaming basket to the Instant Pot.
- Secure the lid and choose the "Manual" button, High pressure and 3 minutes. Once cooking is complete, use a natural release; remove the lid carefully.
- Mash the carrots with a fork or potato masher. Add the butter, paprika, coriander, and heavy cream. Season with salt and black pepper to taste.
- Taste, adjust the seasonings and serve immediately. Bon appétit!

Per serving: 113 Calories; 6g Fat; 14.6g Carbs; 1.5g Protein; 7.3g Sugars

BEANS & GRAINS

40. Easy Vegan Navy Beans

(Ready in about 35 minutes | Servings 6)

INGREDIENTS

1 ¼ pounds dry navy beans
6 cups water
2 tablespoons vegetable bouillon granules
2 bay leaves
1 teaspoon black peppercorns, to taste

DIRECTIONS

- Rinse off and drain the navy beans. Place the navy beans, water, bouillon granules, bay leaves, and black peppercorns in your Instant Pot.
- Secure the lid. Choose the "Manual" mode and cook at High pressure for 20 minutes.
- Once cooking is complete, use a natural release; remove the lid carefully. Bon appétit!

Per serving: 292 Calories; 1.6g Fat; 52.3g Carbs; 19g Protein; 3.6g Sugars

41. Nutty Oatmeal with Figs

(Ready in about 25 minutes | Servings 3)

INGREDIENTS

1 cup steel cut oats
1/2 cup coconut milk
2 tablespoons honey
3 fresh or dried figs, chopped
1/2 cup walnuts, chopped or ground

DIRECTIONS

- Add the steel cut oats, coconut milk, and honey to your Instant Pot. You can add star anise and cinnamon if desired.
- Pour in 2 cups of water
- Secure the lid. Choose the "Manual" mode and High pressure; cook for 10 minutes. Once cooking is complete, use a natural pressure release for 12 minutes; carefully remove the lid.
- Divide the oatmeal among 3 serving bowls; top each serving with chopped figs and walnuts. You can garnish your oatmeal with coconut flakes. Bon appétit!

Per serving: 270 Calories; 13.3g Fat; 43g Carbs; 9.2g Protein; 19.6g Sugars

42. Exotic Oatmeal Breakfast with Walnuts

(Ready in about 25 minutes | Servings 4)

INGREDIENTS

2 cups steel cut oats
1/2 teaspoon ground cinnamon
1/4 teaspoon cardamom
2 bananas
1/2 cup walnuts, chopped

DIRECTIONS

- Add the steel cut oats to your Instant Pot. Sprinkle with cinnamon and cardamom. Pour in 5 ½ cups of water.
- Secure the lid. Choose the "Manual" mode and cook for 10 minutes under High pressure.
- Once cooking is complete, use a natural release for 10 minutes; remove the lid carefully. Ladle into serving bowls.
- Top with bananas and walnuts. Bon appétit!

Per serving: 244 Calories; 10.1g Fat; 48.4g Carbs; 10.4g Protein; 9.2g Sugars

43. Mexican-Style Corn on the Cob

(Ready in about 15 minutes | Servings 3)

INGREDIENTS

3 ears corn on the cob
1/2 stick butter, softened
A few drops of liquid smoke
1/2 lemon, juiced
1 tablespoon fresh cilantro, minced

DIRECTIONS

- Pour 1 ¼ cups of water into the base of your Instant Pot. Place three ears corn on the cob on a metal trivet.
- Secure the lid. Choose the "Steam" mode and cook for 3 minutes under High pressure. Once cooking is complete, use a natural release; remove the lid carefully. Reserve corn on the cob.
- Press the "Sauté" button to heat up your Instant Pot. Melt the butter and remove from heat. Add the liquid smoke, lemon juice, and cilantro; stir to combine.
- Toss the corn on the cob with the smoky lemon butter. Add a pinch of sugar, salt and white pepper to taste. Bon appétit!

Per serving: 263 Calories; 16.2g Fat; 30.9g Carbs; 4.3g Protein; 1.1g Sugars

44. Spicy Bulgur with Pico de Gallo

(Ready in about 25 minutes | Servings 4)

INGREDIENTS

1 yellow onion, chopped
2 garlic cloves, minced
1 ¼ cups bulgur wheat
3 cups roasted vegetable broth
1/2 cup Pico de gallo

DIRECTIONS

- Press the "Sauté" button to preheat your Instant Pot. Heat 2 tablespoons of vegetable oil. Now, sauté the onions with garlic for 1 minute or so.
- Then, stir the bulgur wheat and broth into your Instant Pot. Season with salt, pepper, and paprika to taste.
- Secure the lid. Choose the "Manual" mode and High pressure; cook for 12 minutes. Once cooking is complete, use a natural pressure release for 10 minutes; carefully remove the lid.
- Serve topped with chilled Pico de gallo. Bon appétit!

Per serving: 184 Calories; 10.4g Fat; 17.8g Carbs; 6g Protein; 3.8g Sugars

45. Family Favorite Oatmeal with Almond Butter

(Ready in about 15 minutes | Servings 4)

INGREDIENTS

1 ½ cups regular oats
2 cups almond milk
1 teaspoon cinnamon, ground
2 tablespoons almond butter
1/2 cup chocolate chips

DIRECTIONS

- Simply throw the oats, milk, and cinnamon into the Instant Pot. Pour in 2 cups of water.
- Secure the lid. Choose the "Manual" mode and High pressure; cook for 10 minutes. Once cooking is complete, use a quick pressure release; carefully remove the lid.
- Divide the oatmeal between serving bowls; top with almond butter and chocolate chips. Enjoy!

Per serving: 347 Calories; 12.1g Fat; 51.3g Carbs; 8.7g Protein; 25.1g Sugars

46. Jasmine Rice with Cremini Mushroom

(Ready in about 15 minutes | Servings 5)

INGREDIENTS

2 cups jasmine rice
1 onion, chopped
2 garlic cloves, minced
1/2 pound Cremini mushrooms, thinly sliced

DIRECTIONS

- Rinse the rice under cold running water and transfer to the Instant Pot; add 2 cups of water and 1/4 teaspoon of salt.
- Secure the lid and select the "Manual" mode. Cook at High pressure for 6 minutes. Once cooking is complete, use a natural release; remove the lid carefully.
- Fluff the rice with the rice paddle or fork; reserve.
- Press the "Sauté" button to preheat the Instant Pot; melt 2 tablespoons of butter. Now, sauté the onion until tender and translucent.
- Add the garlic and cook an additional minute or until it is fragrant and lightly browned.
- Add the Cremini mushrooms and continue to sauté until they are slightly browned. Add the reserved jasmine rice, stir and serve warm. Bon appétit!

Per serving: 335 Calories; 14.9g Fat; 60g Carbs; 11g Protein; 2.3g Sugars

47. Creamy Two-Cheese Polenta

(Ready in about 15 minutes | Servings 4)

INGREDIENTS

1 ½ cups cornmeal
1 cup Cheddar cheese, shredded
1/2 cup Ricotta cheese, at room temperature

DIRECTIONS

- Press the "Sauté" button to preheat the Instant Pot. Then, add 6 cups of water and 1/2 stick of butter; bring to a boil.
- Slowly and gradually, whisk in the cornmeal. Season with the salt and pepper.
- Secure the lid. Choose the "Manual" mode and High pressure; cook for 8 minutes. Once cooking is complete, use a natural pressure release; carefully remove the lid.
- Divide between individual bowls; serve topped with cheese. Bon appétit!

Per serving: 502 Calories; 22.1g Fat; 54.2g Carbs; 20.3g Protein; 4.6g Sugars

SNACKS & APPETIZERS

48. Hoisin-Garlic White Mushrooms

(Ready in about 10 minutes | Servings 5)

INGREDIENTS

20 ounces fresh white mushrooms
1/2 cup bottled hoisin sauce
2 garlic cloves, minced
1 teaspoon paprika

DIRECTIONS

- Add all ingredients to your Instant Pot. Season your mushrooms with sea salt and ground black pepper to taste.
- Pour in 1/2 cup of water
- Secure the lid. Choose the "Manual" mode and High pressure; cook for 5 minutes. Once cooking is complete, use a quick pressure release; carefully remove the lid. Remove the mushrooms from the cooking liquid and reserve.
- Then, press the "Sauté" button and continue to simmer until the sauce has reduced and thickened.
- Place the reserved mushrooms in a serving bowl, add the sauce and serve.

Per serving: 124 Calories; 8.1g Fat; 10.2g Carbs; 4.4g Protein; 7.7g Sugars

49. Brussels Sprouts with Butter and Wine

(Ready in about 10 minutes | Servings 4)

INGREDIENTS

2 tablespoons butter
1/2 cup shallots, chopped
1/4 cup dry white wine
1 ½ pounds Brussels sprouts, trimmed and halved

DIRECTIONS

- Press the "Sauté" button to preheat your Instant Pot. Once hot, melt 2 tablespoons of butter and sauté the shallots until tender.
- Add a splash of wine to deglaze the bottom of the Instant Pot. Add the Brussels sprouts to the Instant Pot. Season them with salt and pepper to taste.
- Pour 1 cup of water into your Instant Pot.
- Secure the lid. Choose the "Manual" mode and High pressure; cook for 4 minutes. Once cooking is complete, use a quick pressure release; carefully remove the lid. Bon appétit!

Per serving: 145 Calories; 7.7g Fat; 15.5g Carbs; 7.3g Protein; 3.8g Sugars

50. Easy Sticky Baby Carrots

(Ready in about 15 minutes | Servings 6)

INGREDIENTS

2 ½ pounds baby carrots, trimmed
1 teaspoon thyme
1 teaspoon dill
2 tablespoons coconut oil
1/4 cup honey

DIRECTIONS

- Add 1 ½ cups of water to the base of your Instant Pot.
- Now, arrange the baby carrots in the steaming basket. Transfer the steaming basket to the Instant Pot.
- Secure the lid and choose the "Manual" function; cook for 3 minutes at High pressure. Once cooking is complete, use a quick release; carefully remove the lid.
- Strain the baby carrots and reserve.
- Then, add the other ingredients to the Instant Pot. Press the "Sauté" button and cook until everything is heated through.
- Add the reserved baby carrots. Season with salt and white pepper, and gently stir. Bon appétit!

Per serving: 151 Calories; 4.8g Fat; 28g Carbs; 1.3g Protein; 21.1g Sugars

51. Easy Traditional Hummus

(Ready in about 45 minutes | Servings 8)

INGREDIENTS

1 yellow onion, chopped
2 garlic cloves, minced
1 ½ cups dried chickpeas
3 tablespoons tahini paste
2 tablespoons fresh lemon juice

DIRECTIONS

- Press the "Sauté" button to preheat your Instant Pot. Once hot, heat 1 tablespoon of olive oil until sizzling. Then, cook the onion and garlic until tender and fragrant; reserve.
- Wipe down the Instant Pot with a damp cloth. Then, add the chickpeas and 4 cups of water to the Instant Pot.
- Secure the lid and choose the "Bean/Chili" function; cook for 40 minutes at High pressure. Once cooking is complete, use a natural release; carefully remove the lid.
- Drain the chickpeas, reserving cooking liquid. Now, transfer chickpeas to your blender. Add the tahini, lemon juice, and reserved onion/garlic mixture.
- Process until everything is creamy, uniform, and smooth, adding a splash of cooking liquid. Serve with pita bread and vegetable sticks.

Per serving: 206 Calories; 8.1g Fat; 26.1g Carbs; 8.8g Protein; 4.6g Sugars

52. Movie Night Popcorn with Ranch Butter

(Ready in about 10 minutes | Servings 6)

INGREDIENTS

3/4 cup corn kernels
4 tablespoons butter
1-ounce packet ranch seasoning mix
Sea salt, to taste

DIRECTIONS

- Press the "Sauté" button to preheat your Instant Pot.
- Now, heat 2 tablespoons of olive oil; add corn kernels. Sauté until the corn kernels are well coated with oil.
- Secure the lid and choose the "Manual" function; cook for 5 minutes at High pressure. Once cooking is complete, use a quick release; carefully remove the lid.
- In a saucepan, melt the butter with ranch seasoning mix. Lastly, toss the ranch butter with popcorn; season with salt. Enjoy!

Per serving: 177 Calories; 13.9g Fat; 11.1g Carbs; 2.4g Protein; 3.5g Sugars

53. Hot and Spicy Peanuts

(Ready in about 1 hour 25 minutes | Servings 8)

INGREDIENTS

1 ½ pounds raw peanuts in the shell, rinsed an cleaned

3 jalapenos, sliced

2 tablespoons Creole seasoning

1 teaspoon garlic powder

1 teaspoon lemon pepper

DIRECTIONS

- Place the peanuts in your Instant Pot; add salt and red pepper flakes; cover with water. Add the remaining ingredients and stir to combine.
- Place a trivet on top to hold down the peanuts.
- Secure the lid and choose the "Manual" mode. Cook for 1 hour 20 minutes at High pressure.
- Once cooking is complete, use a natural release; remove the lid carefully. Enjoy!

Per serving: 340 Calories; 28.1g Fat; 13.6g Carbs; 14.1g Protein; 3.6g Sugars

54. Favorite Deviled Eggs

(Ready in about 20 minutes | Servings 8)

INGREDIENTS

8 eggs
3 teaspoons mayonnaise
1 tablespoon sour cream
1 teaspoon gourmet mustard
1/2 teaspoon hot sauce

DIRECTIONS

- Pour 1 ½ cups of water into the base of your Instant Pot.
- Now, arrange the eggs in the steaming basket. Transfer the steaming basket to the Instant Pot.
- Secure the lid and choose the "Manual" function; cook for 13 minutes at Low pressure. Once cooking is complete, use a quick release; remove the lid carefully.
- Peel the eggs under running water. Remove the yolks and smash them with a fork; reserve.
- Now, mix the mayonnaise, sour cream, gourmet mustard, and hot sauce; add reserved yolks and mash everything. Sprinkle the eggs with salt and black pepper.
- Fill the whites with this mixture, heaping it lightly. Garnish with fresh chives and place in the refrigerator until ready to serve. Bon appétit!

Per serving: 138 Calories; 10.4g Fat; 1.2g Carbs; 9.1g Protein; 0.7g Sugars

VEGAN

55. Porridge with Pumpkin and Cherries

(Ready in about 25 minutes | Servings 4)

INGREDIENTS

2 ½ pounds pumpkin, cleaned and seeds removed
1/2 cup rolled oats
4 tablespoons honey
4 tablespoons dried berries

DIRECTIONS

- Add 1 ½ cups of water and a metal trivet to the Instant Pot. Now, place the pumpkin on the trivet.
- Secure the lid. Choose the "Manual" mode and cook for 12 minutes under High pressure. Once cooking is complete, use a natural release; carefully remove the lid.
- Then, purée the pumpkin in the food processor.
- Wipe down the Instant Pot with a damp cloth. Add rolled oats, honey, berries, and pumpkin purée to the Instant Pot, including pumpkin purée. Add 2 cups of water. Add a pinch of salt.
- Secure the lid. Choose the "Manual" mode and cook for 10 minutes under High pressure. Once cooking is complete, use a natural release; carefully remove the lid.
- Sprinkle ground cinnamon and nutmeg over the top of each serving and enjoy!

Per serving: 201 Calories; 1.1g Fat; 51.8g Carbs; 5g Protein; 31.9g Sugars

56. Autumn Barley Bowl

(Ready in about 45 minutes | Servings 4)

INGREDIENTS

2 cloves garlic, minced
1/2 cup scallions, chopped
2 cups butternut squash, peeled and cubed
1/2 teaspoon turmeric powder
2 cups barley, whole

DIRECTIONS

- Press the "Sauté" button to preheat your Instant Pot. Once hot, heat 2 tablespoons of olive oil. Now, cook the garlic and scallions until tender.
- Add the butternut squash, turmeric, and barley; stir to combine. Pour in 4 ½ cups water. Season with sea salt and ground black pepper, to taste.
- Secure the lid. Choose the "Multigrain" mode and cook for 40 minutes under High pressure. Once cooking is complete, use a natural release; carefully remove the lid.
- Ladle into individual bowls and serve warm.

Per serving: 360 Calories; 6.4g Fat; 70g Carbs; 8.7g Protein; 2.2g Sugars

57. Green Beans with Shiitake Mushrooms

(Ready in about 25 minutes | Servings 4)

INGREDIENTS

6 dried shiitake mushrooms
2 cloves garlic, minced
1/2 cup scallions, chopped
1 ½ pounds green beans, fresh or frozen (and thawed)
1 bay leaf

DIRECTIONS

- Press the "Sauté" button and bring 2 cups of water to a rapid boil; remove from the heat; add the dried shiitake mushrooms.
- Allow the mushrooms to sit for 15 minutes to rehydrate. Then cut the mushrooms into slices; reserve the mushroom stock.
- Wipe down the Instant Pot with a kitchen cloth. Press the "Sauté" button to preheat your Instant Pot. Once hot, heat 2 tablespoons of sesame oil.
- Then, sauté the garlic and scallions until tender and aromatic. Add the green beans, bay leaf, and reserved mushrooms and stock; stir to combine well. Season with black pepper, red pepper, and salt.
- Secure the lid. Choose the "Manual" mode and cook for 4 minutes under High pressure. Once cooking is complete, use a quick release; carefully remove the lid. Serve warm.

Per serving: 119 Calories; 7.6g Fat; 12.6g Carbs; 2.6g Protein; 2.6g Sugars

58. Brussels Sprouts with Tomato and Cashews

(Ready in about 15 minutes | Servings 4)

INGREDIENTS

1 pound Brussels sprouts, cut into halves
1/2 cup tomato purée
2 tablespoons soy sauce
1 fresh lime juice
1/4 cup cashew nuts, chopped

DIRECTIONS

- Add the Brussels sprouts and tomato purée to the Instant Pot. Pour in 1 cup of water.
- Sprinkle with salt, black pepper, and cayenne pepper.
- Secure the lid. Choose the "Manual" mode and cook for 4 minutes under High pressure. Once cooking is complete, use a quick release; carefully remove the lid.
- Drizzle soy sauce and lime juice over the top. Add cashew nuts and garnish with fresh cilantro leaves. Serve immediately.

Per serving: 132 Calories; 5.7g Fat; 17.8g Carbs; 6.3g Protein; 5.9g Sugars

59. Mint and Pea Dipping Sauce

(Ready in about 15 minutes | Servings 8)

INGREDIENTS

1 pound dried split peas, rinsed
1 tablespoon fresh lemon juice
4 tablespoons extra-virgin olive oil
1 teaspoon fresh mint, chopped
1/2 teaspoon paprika

DIRECTIONS

- Add the split peas to your Instant Pot. Cover them with 6 cups of water or a homemade vegetable stock.
- Secure the lid. Choose the "Manual" mode and cook for 5 minutes under High pressure. Once cooking is complete, use a natural release; carefully remove the lid.
- Transfer the split peas to your food processor; add lemon juice, olive oil, mint, and paprika. Sprinkle with sea salt and freshly ground black pepper to taste.
- Process until everything is creamy and well combined. Serve well chilled, garnished with fresh parsley. Bon appétit!

Per serving: 79 Calories; 4.5g Fat; 4.4g Carbs; 5.6g Protein; 2.3g Sugars

60. Greek-Style Zucchini with Olives

(Ready in about 15 minutes | Servings 4)

INGREDIENTS

1 garlic clove, minced
1/2 cup scallions, chopped
1 pound zucchinis, sliced
1/2 cup tomato paste
1/2 cup Kalamata olives, pitted and sliced

DIRECTIONS

- Press the "Sauté" button to preheat the Instant Pot. Now, heat 2 tablespoons of garlic-infused olive oil; sauté the garlic and scallions for 2 minutes or until they are tender and fragrant.
- Add the zucchinis and tomato paste; pour in 1 cup of vegetable broth. Sprinkle with salt, black pepper, oregano, basil, and paprika.
- Secure the lid. Choose the "Manual" mode and Low pressure; cook for 4 minutes. Once cooking is complete, use a quick pressure release; carefully remove the lid.
- Serve garnished with Kalamata olives. Bon appétit!

Per serving: 143 Calories; 9.4g Fat; 12.7g Carbs; 5.6g Protein; 4.4g Sugars

61. Goulash with Mushrooms and Chickpeas

(Ready in about 15 minutes | Servings 4)

INGREDIENTS

1 cup scallions, chopped
1 ½ pounds Cremini mushrooms, thinly sliced
2 garlic cloves, smashed
1/4 cup white wine
1 can chickpeas, drained well

DIRECTIONS

- Press the "Sauté" button to preheat the Instant Pot; now, heat 2 tablespoons of peanut oil. Now, cook the scallions until they are tender. Add the mushrooms and garlic; cook for 3 to 4 minutes, stirring periodically.
- Add a splash of white wine to deglaze the pot.
- Season with salt, black pepper, cayenne pepper, dill, and rosemary.
- Secure the lid. Choose the "Manual" mode and High pressure; cook for 10 minutes. Once cooking is complete, use a quick pressure release; carefully remove the lid.
- Add the chickpeas and stir to combine. Divide among serving plates and serve garnished with 1/4 cup of fresh chopped parsley. Bon appétit!

Per serving: 198 Calories; 9.1g Fat; 22.9g Carbs; 10.5g Protein; 6.7g Sugars

DESSERTS

62. The Moistest Chocolate Mug Cakes

(Ready in about 15 minutes | Servings 2)

INGREDIENTS

1/2 cup coconut flour
2 eggs
2 tablespoons honey
1 tablespoon cocoa powder
1 medium-sized mango, peeled and diced

DIRECTIONS

- Combine the coconut flour, eggs, honey, and cocoa powder in two lightly greased mugs. Sprinkle with vanilla and ground nutmeg to taste.
- Then, add 1 cup of water and a metal trivet to the Instant Pot. Lower the uncovered mugs onto the trivet.
- Secure the lid. Choose the "Manual" mode and High pressure; cook for 10 minutes. Once cooking is complete, use a quick pressure release; carefully remove the lid.
- Top with diced mango and serve chilled. Enjoy!

Per serving: 268 Calories; 10.5g Fat; 34.8g Carbs; 10.6g Protein; 31.1g Sugars

63. Indian Kheer with Raisins

(Ready in about 10 minutes | Servings 4)

INGREDIENTS

1 ½ cups basmati rice
3 cups coconut milk
1 teaspoon rosewater
4 tablespoons unsalted pistachios, minced
1/2 cup jaggery

DIRECTIONS

- Add all of the above ingredients to your Instant Pot; sprinkle with a pinch of coarse salt and crushed saffron; stir to combine well.
- Secure the lid. Choose the "Soup" mode and High pressure; cook for 3 minutes. Once cooking is complete, use a natural pressure release; carefully remove the lid.
- Serve topped with 1/2 cup of raisins and enjoy!

Per serving: 408 Calories; 18.7g Fat; 62.4g Carbs; 13.8g Protein; 35.6g Sugars

64. Berry Compote with Rose Wine

(Ready in about 10 minutes | Servings 4)

INGREDIENTS

1 1/3 pounds mixed fresh and dried berries
3/4 cup sugar
1/2 cup rose wine
2 tablespoons fresh orange juice

DIRECTIONS

- Simply throw all of the above ingredients into your Instant Pot. Season with ground cloves, vanilla, and cinnamon.
- Secure the lid. Choose the "Manual" and cook at High pressure for 6 minutes. Once cooking is complete, use a natural release; carefully remove the lid.
- Serve over vanilla ice cream if desired and enjoy!

Per serving: 236 Calories; 0.8g Fat; 61.3g Carbs; 1.1g Protein; 50.2g Sugars

65. Ooey-Gooey Mini Lava Cakes

(Ready in about 20 minutes | Servings 6)

INGREDIENTS

1 stick butter

6 ounces butterscotch morsels

3/4 cup powdered sugar

3 eggs, whisked

7 tablespoons all-purpose flour

DIRECTIONS

- Add 1 ½ cups of water and a metal rack to the Instant Pot. Line a standard-size muffin tin with muffin papers.
- In a microwave-safe bowl, microwave 1 stick of butter and butterscotch morsels for about 40 seconds. Stir in powdered sugar.
- Add eggs and flour. Add vanilla to taste. Spoon the batter into the prepared muffin tin.
- Secure the lid. Choose the "Manual" and cook at High pressure for 10 minutes. Once cooking is complete, use a quick release; carefully remove the lid.
- To remove, let it cool for 5 to 6 minutes. Run a small knife around the sides of each cake and serve. Enjoy!

Per serving: 393 Calories; 21.1g Fat; 45.6g Carbs; 5.6g Protein; 35.4g Sugars

66. Easy Orange Flan

(Ready in about 25 minutes | Servings 4)

INGREDIENTS

2/3 cup muscovado sugar
5 eggs, whisked
25 ounces condensed milk, sweetened
1/4 cup orange juice
1/2 teaspoon pure vanilla extract

DIRECTIONS

- To make a caramel, place sugar in a microwave-safe dish; add 3 tablespoons of water and microwave approximately 3 minutes.
- Now, pour the caramel into four ramekins.
- Then, whisk the eggs with milk, orange juice, and vanilla. Pour the egg mixture into ramekins.
- Add 1 ½ cups of water and a metal rack to the Instant Pot. Now, lower your ramekins onto the rack.
- Secure the lid. Choose the "Manual" and cook at High pressure for 9 minutes. Once cooking is complete, use a natural pressure release for 10 minutes; carefully remove the lid.
- Refrigerate overnight and enjoy!

Per serving: 343 Calories; 17.8g Fat; 28.2g Carbs; 16.9g Protein; 27.4g Sugars

67. Millet Pudding with Dates

(Ready in about 15 minutes | Servings 4)

INGREDIENTS

1 ½ cups millet
1 (14-ounce) can coconut milk
1/2 cup Medjool dates, finely chopped

DIRECTIONS

- Add all of the above ingredients to your Instant Pot; pour in 1 ½ cups of water and stir to combine well.
- Sprinkle with ground cinnamon and cardamom to taste.
- Secure the lid. Choose the "Manual" mode and cook for 1 minute at High pressure. Once cooking is complete, use a natural pressure release for 10 minutes; carefully remove the lid.
- Serve warm or at room temperature.

Per serving: 320 Calories; 3.3g Fat; 63.1g Carbs; 9.3g Protein; 6.7g Sugars

68. Luscious Crème Brûlée

(Ready in about 15 minutes + chilling time | Servings 4)

INGREDIENTS

1 ½ cups double cream
4 egg yolks
1/3 cup Irish cream liqueur
8 tablespoons golden caster sugar

DIRECTIONS

- Start by adding 1 cup of water and a metal rack to your Instant Pot.
- Then, microwave the double cream until thoroughly warmed.
- In a mixing bowl, whisk egg yolks, Irish cream liqueur, 4 tablespoons caster sugar. Add vanilla extract, salt, and nutmeg to taste.
- Gradually add the warm cream, stirring continuously. Spoon the mixture into four ramekins; cover with foil; lower onto the rack.
- Secure the lid. Choose the "Manual" mode and cook for 6 minutes under High pressure. Once cooking is complete, use a natural pressure release; carefully remove the lid.
- Place in your refrigerator for 4 to 5 hours to set. To serve, top each cup with a tablespoon of sugar; use a kitchen torch to melt the sugar and form a caramelized topping. Serve right away.

Per serving: 334 Calories; 25.7g Fat; 20.7g Carbs; 5.6g Protein; 19.9g Sugars

OTHER INSTANT POT FAVORITES

69. Favorite Tagliatelle with Sausage

(Ready in about 10 minutes | Servings 6)

INGREDIENTS

1 pound beef sausage, sliced
1 ½ pounds tagliatelle pasta
2 cups tomato paste
8 ounces Colby cheese, grated
5 ounces Ricotta cheese, crumbled

DIRECTIONS

- Press the "Sauté" button to preheat your Instant Pot. Now, heat 2 teaspoons of canola oil. Cook the sausages until they are no longer pink; reserve.
- Then, stir in the pasta, tomato paste; pour in 3 cups of water. Season with salt and black pepper to taste.
- Secure the lid. Choose the "Manual" mode and High pressure; cook for 4 minutes. Once cooking is complete, use a quick pressure release; carefully remove the lid.
- Next, fold in the cheese; seal the lid and let it sit in the residual heat until heated through. Add the reserved sausage and stir; serve garnished with fresh chives. Bon appétit!

Per serving: 596 Calories; 32.6g Fat; 52.1g Carbs; 26.5g Protein; 11.3g Sugars

70. Traditional Balkan Stew (Satarash)

(Ready in about 35 minutes | Servings 6)

INGREDIENTS

2 pounds beef sirloin steak, cut into bite-sized chunks
1 cup red onion, chopped
1 pound bell peppers, seeded and sliced
4 Italian plum tomatoes, crushed
1 egg, beaten

DIRECTIONS

- Press the "Sauté" button to preheat your Instant Pot. Now, heat 1 tablespoon of olive oil. Cook the beef until it is no longer pink.
- Add the onion and peppers; cook an additional 2 minutes.
- Add the tomatoes and 1 cup of water or a vegetable broth. Season with salt, black pepper, paprika and granulated garlic.
- Secure the lid. Choose the "Soup" mode and High pressure; cook for 20 minutes. Once cooking is complete, use a quick pressure release; carefully remove the lid.
- Afterwards, fold in the egg and stir well; seal the lid and let it sit in the residual heat for 8 to 10 minutes.
- Serve in individual bowls with mashed potatoes. Enjoy!

Per serving: 403 Calories; 21.3g Fat; 16.4g Carbs; 36.8g Protein; 8.7g Sugars

71. Vietnamese Beef Noodle Pho

(Ready in about 15 minutes | Servings 4)

INGREDIENTS

1 pound round steak, sliced paper thin
2 cups mixed winter vegetables
1/2 (14-ounce) package rice noodles
1 bunch of cilantro, roughly chopped
2 stalks scallions, diced

DIRECTIONS

- Press the "Sauté" button to preheat the Instant Pot. Heat 1 tablespoon of sesame oil and sear the round steak for 1 to 2 minutes.
- Add 4 cups of water to the Instant Pot. Season with salt, black pepper, cinnamon and anise. Add the winter vegetables. Top with rice noodles so they should be on top of the other ingredients.
- Secure the lid. Choose the "Manual" mode and High pressure; cook for 3 minutes. Once cooking is complete, use a quick pressure release; carefully remove the lid.
- Serve in individual bowls, topped with cilantro and scallions. Enjoy!

Per serving: 417 Calories; 14g Fat; 27.5g Carbs; 43.1g Protein; 3.6g Sugars

72. Favorite Monkey Bread

(Ready in about 25 minutes | Servings 8)

INGREDIENTS

1 (12-ounce) package biscuit dough, cut in quarters
2/3 cup white sugar
1 teaspoon apple pie spice
1/4 cup coconut oil
1/3 cup brown sugar

DIRECTIONS

- Prepare your Instant Pot by adding 1 cup of water and a metal trivet to its bottom.
- Coat the biscuit dough with white sugar evenly. Arrange the biscuit pieces in a fluted tube pan that is previously greased with a nonstick cooking spray.
- In a mixing bowl, thoroughly combine the apple pie spice, coconut oil, brown sugar; add a pinch of salt; microwave for 40 to 50 seconds or until butter is melted.
- Spread this butter sauce over the biscuit pieces. Place the fluted tube pan onto the trivet; cover the top with a foil.
- Secure the lid. Choose the "Manual" mode and cook for 22 minutes under High pressure. Once cooking is complete, use a natural pressure release; carefully remove the lid. Bon appétit!

Per serving: 283 Calories; 9.1g Fat; 49.2g Carbs; 2.5g Protein; 28.9g Sugars

73. Hot Chocolate Porridge with Banana

(Ready in about 15 minutes | Servings 4)

INGREDIENTS

1 ½ cups steel-cut oats
2 cups chocolate milk
1/3 cup dark chocolate chips
1 large banana, thinly sliced

DIRECTIONS

- Dump the steel-cut oats, chocolate milk, and chocolate chips into your Instant Pot. Pour in 2 cups of water.
- Sprinkle with cinnamon, ginger, and nutmeg (if desired); add a pinch of salt and stir well.
- Secure the lid. Choose the "Manual" mode and cook for 5 minutes under High pressure. Once cooking is complete, use a natural pressure release; carefully remove the lid.
- Taste and adjust the sweetness. Serve in individual bowls topped with sliced banana. Bon appétit!

Per serving: 193 Calories; 6.6g Fat; 37.2g Carbs; 10.3g Protein; 10.8g Sugars

74. Favorite Scrambled Eggs with Ricotta

(Ready in about 10 minutes | Servings 4)

INGREDIENTS

6 whole eggs, beaten
1/2 cup ricotta cheese, crumbled
2 tablespoons fresh parsley leaves, roughly chopped

DIRECTIONS

- Press the "Sauté" button to preheat the Instant Pot. Melt 2 tablespoons of butter and add the beaten eggs.
- Season the eggs with salt, black pepper and paprika to your liking; stir to combine well. Scramble the eggs in the Instant Pot using a wide spatula. Add the ricotta cheese and stir until heated through.
- Secure the lid. Choose the "Manual" mode and cook for 5 minutes under High pressure. Once cooking is complete, use a quick pressure release; carefully remove the lid.
- Divide between serving plates; top with fresh chopped parsley and serve warm. Bon appétit!

Per serving: 205 Calories; 16.1g Fat; 2.7g Carbs; 12.1g Protein; 0.9g Sugars

75. Eggs with Cheese and Toasted Bread

(Ready in about 15 minutes | Servings 6)

INGREDIENTS

6 eggs
6 tablespoons Feta cheese
6 slices toasted bread
Salt, to taste
1/2 teaspoon paprika

DIRECTIONS

- Place 1 ½ cups of water and a steamer basket in the bottom of the Instant Pot. Add the eggs to the steamer basket.
- Secure the lid. Choose the "Manual" mode. Cook for 7 minutes at High pressure. Once cooking is complete, use a quick release; carefully remove the lid.
- Season your eggs with salt and paprika. Spread feta cheese on toasted bread. Serve with eggs and enjoy!

Per serving: 227 Calories; 13.5g Fat; 12.3g Carbs; 13.2g Protein; 2.9g Sugars

19857046R00052

Made in the USA
Lexington, KY
30 November 2018